LAURA INGALLS *Wilder*

SPIRIT
of America®

LAURA INGALLS *Wilder*

PIONEER AND AUTHOR

By Judy Alter

*Content Adviser: Cheryl Palmlund, Laura Ingalls Wilder Memorial Society,
De Smet, South Dakota*

The Child's World®
Chanhassen, Minnesota

Laura Ingalls *Wilder*

Published in the United States of America by The Child's World®
PO Box 326 • Chanhassen, MN 55317-0326 • 800-599-READ • www.childsworld.com

Acknowledgments
The Child's World®: Mary Berendes, Publishing Director

Editorial Directions, Inc.: E. Russell Primm, Editorial Director; Pam Rosenberg, Line Editor; Elizabeth K. Martin, Assistant Editor; Olivia Nellums, Editorial Assistant; Susan Hindman, Copy Editor; Susan Ashley, Halley Gatenby, Proofreaders; Jean Cotterell, Kevin Cunningham, Peter Garnham, Fact Checkers; Tim Griffin/IndexServ, Indexer; Dawn Friedman, Photo Researcher; Linda S. Koutris, Photo Selector

Photo
Cover: Rose Wilder Lane Collection, Herbert Hoover Library; Corbis: 13; Tim Thompson/Corbis: 14; Bettmann/Corbis: 18, 19, 28; David Muench/Corbis: 25; Buddy Mays/Corbis: 26; Rose Wilder Lane Collection, Herbert Hoover Library: 2, 10, 16; copyright Little House Heritage Trust, all rights reserved, and Rose Wilder Lane Collection, Herbert Hoover Library: 11; DeWitt Ward/Rose Wilder Lane Collection, Herbert Hoover Library: 27; Laura Ingalls Wilder Home Association, Mansfield, MO: 6, 7, 20, 22, 23, 24; Laura Ingalls Wilder Memorial Society, Inc., DeSmet, SD: 8; North Wind Picture Archives: 9, 12, 15, 17; Brad Mogen /Visuals Unlimited, Inc.: 21.

Library of Congress Cataloging-in-Publication Data
Alter, Judy, 1938–
 Laura Ingalls Wilder : pioneer and author / by Judy Alter.
   p. cm.— (Our people)
 "Spirit of America."
 Includes index.
 Contents: Child of pioneers—A home in De Smet—A new life for Laura—A career in writing.
  ISBN 1-59296-007-3 (Library Bound : alk. paper)
 1. Wilder, Laura Ingalls, 1867–1957—Juvenile literature. 2. Authors, American—20th century—
Biography—Juvenile literature. 3. Women pioneers—United States—Biography—Juvenile literature.
4. Frontier and pioneer life—United States—Juvenile literature. 5. Children's stories—Authorship—
Juvenile literature. [1. Wilder, Laura Ingalls, 1867–1957. 2. Authors, American. 3. Women—Biography.] I. Title. II. Series.
 PS3545.I342Z553 2004
 813'.52—dc21   2003004256

14   18   28

Contents

Chapter ONE

Child of Pioneers

Laura Ingalls (right) with her sisters Carrie and Mary

LAURA INGALLS WILDER GREW UP AT A TIME when the United States itself was growing. As an adult, Laura wrote books about life as a **pioneer.** She based them on the experiences of her family. She never imagined that her books would bring fame to her family and bring the history of the American West alive for readers for years to come.

Laura was born February 7, 1867, near Pepin, Wisconsin. She was the second child born to Charles and Caroline Ingalls. Laura's sister, Mary, was two years older. They called their parents Pa and Ma. The Ingalls family lived in a log cabin in the "Big Woods," 7 miles (11 kilometers) from the town. Charles hunted for mink, muskrat, fox, deer, and bear. Caroline smoked the meat. They grew corn, oats, turnips, pumpkins, potatoes, and carrots.

Charles and Caroline Ingalls were Laura's parents.

The trees and rocky soil of Wisconsin made farming hard work. Charles longed for the open prairies out West. Laura was just a toddler in 1869 when the family moved to Kansas. They traveled by covered wagon across eastern Minnesota. They passed through Iowa and Missouri and finally stopped in Kansas. Everything they owned was in the wagon. It held clothes, dishes, bedding, keepsakes, Caroline's books, and Charles's fiddle. They crossed dangerous rivers. Sometimes, they did not see other people for days. Some days, it

Interesting Fact

▶ Charles Ingalls was born in New York, but his family moved west until they finally settled in Wisconsin. He was self-educated and wise in the ways of the woods. He was known as a great storyteller.

rained heavily. On other days, the hot sun beat down on them. At night, they camped and built a fire. Charles played his fiddle. Laura loved to hear him play.

Charles settled his family in Rutland Township in Montgomery County. He built a house and a log stable, dug a well, and plowed the prairie so he could plant crops. Laura's sister Carrie was born while the family lived in Kansas. But Charles didn't realize he was on land that belonged to the Osage, a Native American group. The Osage became angry with the settlers who were taking their land. The U.S. government paid the Osage to move further west. Then, when Laura was four, the Ingalls family also moved. They went back to the cabin in the Wisconsin woods.

In 1874, the family packed their wagon again. This time, they settled in Minnesota. Charles bought farmland near the town of Walnut Grove. He planned to raise wheat to ship to mills in St. Paul. The family lived in a **dugout.** Laura went to school for the first

Carrie Ingalls, Laura's sister, was born in Kansas.

Interesting Fact

▶ Caroline Quiner Ingalls was born in Wisconsin. She was one of seven children in a pioneer family. Her father died when she was young. Nearby American Indians brought food to the family. Caroline was well educated. Before she married Charles, she taught school.

8

time. She liked school and learned quickly.

Charles built his family a wooden house with glass windows and factory-made doors. He thought the wheat crop would pay for the house. But swarms of grasshoppers ate his wheat crop two years in a row. He had to leave his family for long periods of time to work as a harvester in eastern Minnesota. It was a difficult time for Laura's family. Then, in 1875, Charles Frederick was born. The family experienced even more **hardship** when little Freddie died only nine months later.

The family hoped for better luck when they moved to Burr Oak, Iowa. For a while, Charles and Caroline helped run a hotel owned by friends. Laura and Mary helped, too. They made beds, washed dishes, waited on tables, and babysat. Laura went to school again. Charles and Caroline's last daughter, Grace,

A dugout built into the side of a hill on the prairie

was born in Burr Oak. But Charles missed living in the country. He moved his family back to Walnut Grove.

In 1879, illness hit the family. No one knows exactly what the sickness was. They all recovered, but Mary went blind. Laura became her sister's eyes. She helped her with schoolwork and described everything she saw to Mary.

Charles was not making enough money by farming to support a family of six. He took a job as an innkeeper and paymaster for the railroad. Though it was hard to make ends meet, he still hoped to own his own land on the **frontier** someday. The opportunity came in 1879 when he was offered a job in Dakota Territory for $50 a month. He would be the timekeeper and the paymaster for the railroad as it pushed into the West.

Mary Ingalls went blind in 1879, the year the Ingalls family suffered an unknown illness.

AT HER DEATH, LAURA INGALLS WILDER DID NOT LEAVE MUCH information about her life. There was one diary, written when she moved to Missouri in 1894. A few letters to and from her daughter, Rose, survived. There were a few other bits of written materials. Records do exist of her community activities and the many newspaper columns she wrote about life in the country. Much of what we know about her life comes from her novels.

But her books do not tell everything that happened in Laura's life. "I lived everything told of in the Little House books, but I did not write all the truth," Laura said. Several years are missing between the books *On the Banks of Plum Creek* and *By the Shores of Silver Lake.*

> 1/26, 1939
>
> Rose Dearest
>
> You must, I think, be in your apartment by this time, so we are sending an express pkg. to 550 East Sixteenth street.
>
> Evidently you have no mail box there yet or I would have had word of it.
>
> I have used up all my excuses etc. and think I will just not answer this letter. She can think I have gone to Timbuctoo or am sick or mad or just to lazy to write
>
> We have had two snows that were so deep, 10 in. once and then 7 in., that we could not get up the hill with the car, if we had gone down so we didn't go down for two weeks or more, I lose my breath if I walk down the hill, so I dont do that not even for the mail and the house is getting awfully stale.
>
> We are all right and comfortable waiting for spring to come.
>
> Much love
>
> Mama Bess

Those were difficult years for her family. Another reason she did not write about that time was that the family had to move to Iowa, which was more settled than Kansas and the Dakota Territory. Laura wanted her books to show the joys and struggles of her family as pioneers on the American frontier.

11

Chapter TWO

A Home in De Smet

THE UNITED STATES WAS GROWING, AND settlers were moving further west. As people moved west, so did the railroad. New tracks were being built on the prairies of Dakota Territory. Charles arrived there ahead of Caroline and the girls, who were too ill to travel. That summer, when they recovered, they traveled by train to Tracy, Minnesota. Laura enjoyed her first train ride.

Charles met them in Tracy with the wagon and took

As settlers pushed into the western U.S. territories, the railroad followed.

them the rest of the way to the Silver Lake railroad camp. That fall, the family was offered the **surveyors'** house for the winter. The family moved right in. Soon,

A group of railroad surveyors in Dakota Territory

the town of De Smet would grow on the shores of Silver Lake. The Ingalls family was considered the "first family" of De Smet because they had spent that winter on the Dakota prairie.

As the railroad moved westward, it left newly built towns behind it. By 1880, settlers were crowding the prairie. The Ingalls served meals and rented sleeping space to newcomers who had nowhere else to stay. Meals were twenty-five cents, and a place on the floor for the night was twenty-five cents. The town grew quickly. By the spring of 1880, there were 16 buildings and a newspaper.

Interesting Fact

▶ The town of De Smet was named after Father De Smet, a French priest much loved by American Indians.

The Ingalls family stayed in the new town. Charles built a **shanty** for them on a **homestead** a mile from town. The whole family helped dig a well, build a barn for the horses and cattle, plow the prairie, and plant the garden. Laura took Mary for walks and described their new home to her.

In the fall of 1880, an old Native American man predicted that the winter would be severe. Charles believed the man's prediction

The Ingalls family spent their first winter on Silver Lake in this house.

and moved the family into town to live at his store on Main Street. The old man was right. That winter the town suffered many **blizzards.** Laura and Carrie nearly lost their way coming home from school during one of them. Then school was canceled.

Blizzards made life on the prairie difficult during the winter.

Charles and other men in town had to clear snow from the railroad tracks so that the train could bring supplies. In January, the railroad company announced that trains would not run again until spring. Snow and ice had drifted across the tracks, and trains could not get through.

Supplies in De Smet ran low. The trains could not bring coal, so people burned lumber and hay to keep warm. The townspeople were afraid they would not have anything to eat. Two men made a dangerous trip across the prairie. They bought wheat from a homesteader about 20 miles (32 kilometers) away so that the people of De Smet could make flour for bread. They were lucky not to get

Interesting Fact

▶ The 1862 Homestead Act said that any American citizen over age 21 could claim 160 acres (65 hectares) of land in certain territories west of the Mississippi River. The homesteader had to build a house, live in it for six months of the year, and plow the land so there would be a crop. Then after five years, the homesteader would own the property.

lost on the prairie in the blizzard. One of these brave men was Cap Garland, a boy in Laura's class at school. The other was a homesteader named Almanzo Wilder.

Almanzo Wilder was one of the two brave men who made a trip across the prairie in the snow to bring supplies back to the town of DeSmet.

BLIZZARDS WERE A REAL DANGER ON THE PRAIRIE. EVEN IN GOOD WEATHER, it was hard to find your way. The prairie looked the same whatever way you turned. It has been compared to a huge sea of grass. Settlers learned to recognize landmarks, such as a slight rise in the ground or a difference in the grass. But in a blizzard, no one could see these signposts. People had been known to get lost and freeze to death between their homes and their barns. Wise settlers strung a rope from the house to the barn. They followed the rope to keep from getting lost.

Some of Laura Ingalls Wilder's books described how settlers learned to survive if they got lost in a blizzard. They could dig into a haystack on the prairie to stay warm. Or they could find shelter under a stream bank walled in by the snow. That's what Pa did in *On the Banks of Plum Creek* when a blizzard came up while he was walking home from town. He survived by eating the crackers and candy he was bringing home for Christmas.

Chapter THREE

Changes for Laura

LAURA WORKED IN TOWN MAKING SHIRTS TO help with expenses. She didn't like working in town. But the Ingalls family wanted to send Mary to a special college for the blind in Vinton, Iowa. Laura wanted to help send Mary to college.

Laura was only 15 when she was asked to teach for two months at a school 12 miles (19.3 kilometers) away. She taught at the Bouchie School and boarded with the Bouchie family. Her

Students at a rural elementary school in the late 1800s

Laura Ingalls was a 17-year-old teacher when this picture was taken.

first teaching job was challenging. One of her students was older than she was. Laura also did not like living with the Bouchies. But every weekend, Almanzo Wilder came to take her back to De Smet.

Almanzo was 10 years older than Laura. He had moved to Dakota Territory with his brother Royal. Laura told him that once she moved back home, she would not ride with him anymore. Still, after she returned to De Smet, he kept asking her to go on sleigh rides

Interesting Fact

▶ Almanzo Wilder was born on February 13, 1857. His family lived in Malone, New York at the time. The Wilder family moved to Springfield, Minnesota in 1875.

19

in the winter and buggy rides in the spring. Finally, she agreed to ride with him. Laura soon began calling him by a shortened name, Manly.

In 1884, Laura had another teaching job closer to home. There were only three students at the school. On weekends, she worked for a seamstress in De Smet. She used the extra money to buy patterns and material and hats for church. Laura continued to go on buggy rides with Manly. That summer, Manly gave her an engagement ring.

Laura heard that Manly's family was planning on being part of a big wedding. She knew that her father could not afford a big wedding. So, they went to the minister's house and were married on August 25, 1885. After the wedding, they had dinner with her

Laura Ingalls and Almanzo Wilder at their wedding

family. Then the newlyweds rode across the prairie to the house Manly had built for them.

Laura was now a home-steader's wife. Almanzo had a homestead claim and a tree claim.

Hail can ruin a farmer's crops. These cornstalks have been badly damaged by a hailstorm.

He had built Laura a gray house on his tree claim, which was land that had cottonwood, box elder, and elm trees on it. Laura and Manly began to farm, but it was difficult. Laura received only five cents a dozen for the eggs she sent to town. She couldn't sell her butter at all. They didn't have the machinery to farm the land efficiently. Manly **mortgaged** the house to buy machinery. Laura didn't want Manly to pay hired help. She learned to run the machinery they bought.

In 1886, a summer hailstorm ruined their crops. Laura and Manly had to close the house and move to a shanty on the homestead

Interesting Fact

▶ Laura Ingalls was re-luctant to marry Almanzo Wilder because marriage meant she would have to stop teaching. Mar-ried women were not allowed to teach.

claim. The winter brought them joy, however. Their daughter, Rose, was born on December 5, 1886. The next year, crops were poor again because of hot winds and dry weather. Their hay crop and barn burned. In 1888, Laura and Manly both came down with **diphtheria.** Rose stayed with Laura's parents while Manly's brother nursed the couple back to health. But Manly never fully recovered. His health was a problem for the rest of his life. He was not able to do hard work on the farm as he had once done. The family moved back to the tree claim and sold the homestead.

Drought again ruined the crops the following summer. In August, Laura gave birth to a baby boy, who lived only a few days. Not long after that, Rose was feeding hay sticks into the stove when the kitchen caught fire. She had only minor burns, but their house was destroyed. In the spring of 1890, Laura, Manly, and Rose left for Minnesota where Manly's family lived.

Rose Wilder was born in 1866. This picture was taken when she was four years old.

LAURA INGALLS WILDER'S NOVELS CHRONICLE HER LIFE. THE FIRST BOOK, *Little House in the Big Woods,* is about life in Wisconsin when Laura was a little girl. Her novel, *Farmer Boy,* tells of Manly's early life. *Little House on the Prairie* is about life in Kansas. Laura was only a few years old when her family lived in Kansas. She based the book mostly on her family's stories. *On the*

Banks of Plum Creek is about life in Walnut Grove. It is the first book in which Laura shows her family as part of a community. She did not write a novel about their experiences in Burr Oak, Iowa.

By the Shores of Silver Lake is the first novel about De Smet. The railroad camp at De Smet was on the shore of a prairie lake called Silver Lake. The second De Smet novel, *The Long Winter,* introduces Manly. It tells the story of how the Ingalls family and the town survived the hard winter of 1881. The last two Little House books are *Little Town on the Prairie* and *These Happy Golden Years.* These books take place when Laura was older. They describe her as a student and then as a teacher. They also tell of her friendship with Manly.

When Laura died, she left behind the manuscript for a book she never finished. It was published after Rose's death in 1968. *The First Four Years* tells the story of Laura and Manly's first years of marriage.

Chapter FOUR

A Career in Writing

Laura Ingalls Wilder, age 25

LAURA BEGAN A PERIOD OF MOVING FROM place to place as her parents had once done. The Wilders went to Florida, hoping that the warm weather would help Manly's health. But it didn't. The dampness and heat also made Laura sick. They went back to De Smet. Manly worked as a carpenter or in his brother's store when he could. Laura again worked for the seamstress in town.

Manly's poor health meant they could not work on their homestead. They realized that De Smet was not the place to make a living without a homestead. In 1894, Manly, Laura, and Rose moved again. (Laura kept a diary of their journey, which was published after her death.) The family settled in Mansfield, Missouri, a little town in the **Ozark Mountains.** The lovely, green Ozarks were so different from the dusty Dakota prairie. The family would have better luck here. Mansfield would become their final stop.

They bought a farm with a small log cabin in the rocky hills. Laura named their home Rocky Ridge Farm. Manly was still too weak to work the farm by himself. Laura helped him clear brush and trees and build fence rails, a log barn, and a henhouse. They planted a few crops and an apple orchard. Laura sold hens and eggs. They sold firewood from trees on their farm. Still, they did not have much money.

The lovely, green of the Ozark Mountain region was a welcome sight to the Wilders when they arrived.

The town of Mansfield was growing. When the railroad came, new families and industries moved in. Laura and Manly also moved to town, renting a little white house. Laura served meals to the railroad workers. Manly became a **drayman** for the railroad. Several years later, Laura and Manly moved back to the farm. They continued to work

Interesting Fact

▶ In a railroad store in the late 1870s, overalls cost $1.00; a shirt was seventy cents; boots were $4.40; suspenders were thirty-five cents; a loaf of bread was ten cents; and a sack of flour was $2.10.

The Wilders lived in this house on Rocky Ridge Farm, near Mansfield, Missouri.

hard. Manly turned their log cabin into a real house.

Laura and Manly made sure that Rose went to school in Mansfield. Rose later went to live with Manly's sister in Louisiana and finished high school there. Through the years, Manly's family visited several times. So did Laura's sister Carrie.

Laura was very successful at raising hens. She was often invited to speak at farm meetings. The editor of *The Missouri Ruralist* asked her to submit an article. She wrote "Favors the Small Farm Home." The editor asked for more pieces. She wrote interviews with country people, essays, poems, and feature stories. Soon, she began to write for other magazines, including *McCall's* and *The Country Gentleman.*

By 1915, Rose was living in California and working as a **journalist.** Laura went to California for two months to visit her. During World War I, Rose traveled all over Europe as a reporter. She wrote postcards home to her parents in Missouri. Readers all over the United States read her articles in magazines. In 1923, Rose moved back to Rocky Ridge Farm for a few years. Her writing inspired Laura to expand her own writing.

Laura had been a farmer's daughter and a farmer's wife. Now she became a writer. She decided to write an **autobiography** and call it *Pioneer Girl*. With Rose's help, she sent it to a publisher. An editor at Alfred A. Knopf publishing house suggested that Laura tell just the story of her childhood. He also said to change the title. The result was *Little House in the Big Woods*. Harper and Brothers published the book in 1932. Laura decided to write a series. She wrote the Little House books during the next 11 years. She was 77 years old when she finished the last one, *These Happy Golden Years*.

Laura's books told the story of pioneers in the American West. But soon, children all around the world were reading about the Ingalls family. They wrote her many letters. Laura answered all of them. A few years after World War II, she received a letter from **refugee** children in Germany. They told Laura they liked her books because they too had lived through difficult times. They wrote, "We like the books in which

Rose Wilder Lane was a successful journalist.

27

people try to live within bad circumstances; and not only to live, but to be cheerful and brave."

Laura's books brought her fame. Sometimes she had to travel to other states. But she continued to live a quiet life in Mansfield. Manly died in October 1949. Laura stayed at Rocky Ridge after his death. Rose visited her often. Laura Ingalls Wilder died in 1957, three days after her 90th birthday. But to her readers, she is still the young Laura of her books. The *Little House* books continue to bring to life the troubles and joys of families on the American frontier.

Laura Ingalls Wilder's books continue to bring the American frontier to life for many readers.

1867　Laura is born in the "Big Woods" near Pepin, Wisconsin.

1869　The Ingalls family moves to Kansas. Carrie is born while the family lives in Kansas.

1871　The family moves back to Pepin.

1874　The family moves to Walnut Grove, Minnesota.

1876　Laura's nine-month-old brother, Freddie, dies. The family moves to Burr Oak, Iowa.

1878　The family returns to Walnut Grove with new baby Grace.

1879　The Ingalls family is hit by an unknown illness. Mary loses her eyesight. The family settles near the railroad camp of De Smet on the shores of Silver Lake in the Dakota Territory.

1885　Laura Ingalls marries Almanzo (Manly) Wilder.

1886　Laura and Manly Wilder's daughter, Rose, is born.

1888　Laura and Manly become ill with diphtheria.

1889　Laura gives birth to a son, who dies after a few days. Their house burns down.

1890　The Wilders leave De Smet for Minnesota to stay with Manly's family.

1894　After a brief stay in Florida and a return to De Smet, the Wilders move to Mansfield, Missouri.

1902　Charles Ingalls dies on June 8 in De Smet.

1908　Rose Wilder moves to San Francisco, California.

1909　Rose Wilder marries Gillette Lane. This marriage ends in divorce less than 10 years later.

1915　Laura Ingalls Wilder travels to California to visit Rose.

1924　Caroline Ingalls dies on April 20 in De Smet.

1932　Harper and Brothers publishes *Little House in the Big Woods*.

1949　Manly dies at Rocky Ridge Farm.

1954　The Laura Ingalls Wilder Award is established. It is an award given to an author or illustrator whose books contribute greatly to children's literature. Laura was the first author to receive this award.

1957　Laura dies at her home in Mansfield, Missouri.

autobiography (aw-toh-bye-OG-ruh-fee)
An autobiography is the true story about the life of a person that is written by that person. Laura Ingalls Wilder wrote an autobiography and called it Pioneer Girl.

blizzards (BLIZ-zurds)
Blizzards are heavy snowstorms accompanied by cold temperatures and very strong wind. The Ingalls family survived many blizzards during the winter of 1880–1881.

diphtheria (dif-THIR-ee-uh)
Diphtheria is a highly contagious infection that sometimes causes death. Symptoms include difficulty in breathing, high fever, and weakness. Laura and Manly Wilder were stricken with diphtheria in 1888.

drayman (DRAY-man)
A drayman loads and unloads railroad cars or drives a heavy cart called a dray. Manly Wilder worked as a drayman for the railroad.

dugout (DUHG-out)
A dugout is a shelter that is dug out of the ground or the side of a hill. Laura's family lived in a dugout in Minnesota.

frontier (fruhn-TEER)
The edge of a country that is still not settled is called the frontier. The Ingalls family lived on the frontier.

hardship (HARD-ship)
A hardship is something that is difficult or causes suffering. The Ingalls family experienced great hardship when little Freddie died.

homestead (HOME-sted)
An area of land given by the government is called a homestead. A homesteader lives on the homestead.

journalist (JUR-nuhl-ist)
A journalist collects, writes, edits, and publishes news in newspapers or magazines. Rose Wilder became a successful journalist.

mortgaged (MOR-gijd)
If something is mortgaged, it has been used to get a loan. Manly Wilder mortgaged the house so that he and Laura could buy farm machinery.

Ozark Mountains (OH-zark MOUN-tuhnz)
The Ozark Mountains are made up of rolling hills and low mountains, freshwater springs and rivers. They are found in northern Arkansas, southern Missouri, eastern Kansas, and Oklahoma. The Wilders settled in Mansfield, Missouri, a little town in the Ozark Mountains.

pioneer (pye-uh-NEER)
A pioneer explores and settles a new place. Laura Ingalls Wilder was a pioneer.

refugee (ref-yuh-JEE)
A person who has been forced to leave home, often because of war, is a refugee. Refugee children in Germany wrote to Laura Ingalls Wilder after World War II.

shanty (SHAN-tee)
A shanty is a roughly built cabin or a shack. Charles Ingalls built a shanty on his homestead.

surveyor (sur-VAY-ur)
A surveyor makes a living measuring land and marking boundaries. The Ingalls family lived in the surveyors' house for the winter.

Web Sites

Visit our homepage for lots of links about Laura Ingalls Wilder:
http://www.childsworld.com/links.html

Note to Parents, Teachers, and Librarians:
We routinely verify our Web links to make sure they're safe,
active sites—so encourage your readers to check them out!

Books

Anderson, William. *Laura Ingalls Wilder, a Biography.* New York: HarperCollins, 1992.

Wade, Mary Dodson. *Homesteading on the Plains: Daily Life in the Land of Laura Ingalls Wilder.* Brookfield, Conn.: Millbrook Press, 1997.

Wilder, Laura Ingalls. *On the Way Home: The Diary of a Trip from South Dakota to Mansfield, Missouri, in 1894.* New York: HarperCollins, 1962.

Wilder, Laura Ingalls, and William Anderson (commentary). *The Laura Ingalls Wilder Country Cookbook.* New York: HarperCollins, 1995.

Places to Visit or Contact

Laura Ingalls Wilder Memorial Society
To write for more information about visiting the surveyors' house where the Ingalls lived and other sites in De Smet
P.O. Box 426
De Smet, SD 57231
800/880-3383

Laura Ingalls Wilder/Rose Wilder Lane Historic Home and Museum
To visit Rocky Ridge Farm, the Wilder home in Mansfield
3068 Highway A
Mansfield, MO 65704
417/924-3626

Index

About the Author

JUDY ALTER IS THE AUTHOR OF MORE THAN 30 BOOKS, BOTH FICTION AND nonfiction. Her nonfiction books for young readers include Spirit of America®: Our People biographies of Daniel Boone, Sacagawea, Christopher Columbus, and Samuel F. B. Morse, as well as Mexican Americans in the Spirit of America®: Our Cultural Heritage series. Ms. Alter is the director of a small university publishing division. She has four children—all grown—two cats, and a large dog. She enjoys cooking, reading, and gardening.